MW01269044

THIS JOURNAL BELONGS TO:

CHECK OUT ALL OF OUR
WATERCOLOR DOG JOURNALS SERIES

COLLEGE-RULED LINED JOURNALS
amazon.com/gp/product/B094NQWSPR

DOT GRID JOURNAL NOTEBOOKS
amazon.com/gp/product/B094NTJ2BS

amazon.com/gp/product/B08S2NFGZQ

CHECK OUT ALL OF OUR
WATERCOLOR CAT JOURNALS SERIES

COLLEGE-RULED LINED JOURNALS
amazon.com/gp/product/B094Q4BBGV

DOT GRID JOURNAL NOTEBOOKS
amazon.com/gp/product/B094R92SQT

amazon.com/gp/product/B08SFVPXH4

LOVE IT?
Buy it again or get one for yourself!

Hello and thank you for purchasing this book. We hope you have enjoyed using it as much as we enjoyed designing it. We are a small husband and wife business. Words cannot express how much we appreciate that you bought our book.

It would help us a lot if you could take a moment and leave a review about this book on Amazon.

Pet Lovers Universe